Keto Mexican Rice and Low-Carb Meals

Easy Keto Mexican Rice Recipe and More to Help You Lose Weight and Stay Healthy

By: Amy Moore

financial, medical or professional advice. The content within this book has been derived from various sources. Please consult a licensed professional before attempting any techniques outlined in this book.

By reading this document, the reader agrees that under no circumstances is the author responsible for any losses, direct or indirect, that are incurred as a result of the use of information contained within this document, including, but not limited to, errors, omissions, or inaccuracies.

Table of Contents

Introduction

Naturally, as human beings, we all have this innate desire to be the best version of ourselves. This is why the process of self-improvement seems to be a never-ending journey. And the fact that you're reading this means that you have taken it upon yourself to embark on this journey as well. So, perhaps a congratulations is in order for you. You are one of the special people in this world who have decided that good is not good enough. You want to be your best self. And that is precisely why you have made the decision to try to better yourself in whatever way you can.

Of course, human life and existence can be very complex. However, you don't have to stress and tire yourself when trying to achieve your goals and dreams. There are various resources and tools that you can make use of to help you get to where you need to be. This book can be used as one of those tools. If you are taking an active interest in reading this book, then it would be safe to assume that you are someone who is looking to lose weight through the keto diet. While losing weight and staying healthy may not be the easiest things to do in the world, there is still a way to make the process enjoyable and fulfilling.

One of the biggest challenges that people on diets face is the fact that the diet can become boring and repetitive. Part of what makes not being on a diet so appealing is the fact that there is so much freedom. There are no restrictions. You get to eat whatever you want and as much of it as you desire. However, truth be told, there are just far too many of us who abuse this kind of freedom. This is the reason why so many people end up getting obese. They overindulge on food and they eat more than is necessary. Hence, the obesity epidemic that plagues our world today. What a dietary program is, is it provides structure and order to one's food consumption habits. But again, the problem lies in diets becoming too boring and repetitive.

Whenever that's the case, it can make these diets become unsustainable as well.

This book is going to serve as the antidote to that problem. You will come to discover that diets don't always have to be that way. Staying healthy and fit doesn't always have to mean you have to be miserable and bored with food. There is still a lot of fun to be had in the process of getting fit. It's just a matter of you getting creative and exposing yourself to the many ways you can spice things up in your diet...literally.

However, before we start getting into the nitty-gritty details of the recipes, perhaps it would be best for you to have a little refresher on how the keto diet works and the specific things that you need to be looking out for while you're on a diet.

How Keto Works

Keto is a popular diet these days that plenty of people have developed some level of familiarity with. There's no denying the fact that it's one of the most popular dietary programs in the world today. There are all sorts of specialized restaurants that offer keto-friendly dishes. There are numerous cookbooks on the market that are geared especially toward keto-friendly recipes. While the history of the keto diet is a long and storied one, you don't really need to familiarize yourself with all of that. All you need to know is that this is a diet that promotes a high consumption of fat, moderate consumption of protein, and minimal consumption of carbohydrates.

The way that the keto diet works is that it promotes the high production of ketones within the body. Normally, the body relies on carbohydrates to produce energy. The carbohydrates that are eaten are converted into glucose. Then, that glucose is broken down to serve as energy which is used to carry out normal body processes. Any leftover glucose is converted into stored body fat that will be used for future physical activity.

What the keto diet does is that it limits the consumption of carbohydrates. And what that means is that the body doesn't rely on the glucose from carbohydrates for energy anymore. Instead, it turns towards alternative sources of fuel and energy in order to sustain healthy bodily function and movement. In order to make up for the lack of carbohydrates, the liver breaks down stored fat and produces ketones, which are then used to provide energy for the body. Since the stored fat is broken down to sustain physical activity, the ketogenic diet then makes the weight loss process more efficient and effective.

By limiting the amount of carbohydrates that you consume and by upping your fat intake, you are thereby entering your body into a ketogenic state. And when you enter this state, you are forcing your body to burn stored fat to help you lose weight more effectively.

Tips for Making Keto Work

Of course, while the premise of the keto diet might seem simple enough, it's still not something that you want to be going into too nonchalantly. There are still a few tips and tricks that you will want to keep in mind in order for you to maximize the diet and follow it properly. After all, when it comes to your health and wellness, you always want to be paying attention to all the details surrounding your diet to make sure that you're doing it right.

Cook Your Own Food

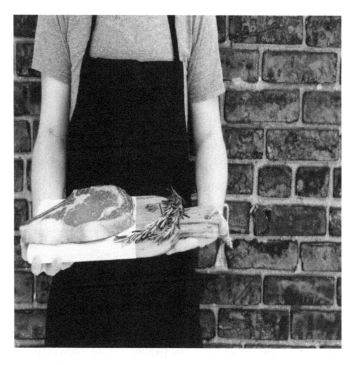

Even though cooking might not necessarily be an activity that falls into your comfort zone, it's going to be very beneficial if you cook your own food yourself. This is the only way that you can truly know what you're putting into your mouth and how much of it you're consuming. If you eat out, then you are essentially at the mercy of the people who cook your food for you. There's no telling how much of each ingredient they might be putting into your meal. And this can result in a lot of hidden calories and nutrients that could prove to be counterproductive to your diet.

Keep Track of Your Macros

It's true that the keto diet is one that primarily promotes the high consumption of fat and the minimal consumption of carbohydrates. However, while the premise might seem simplistic, it's still important to really get into the numbers. The best way to make sure that you are putting your body in a ketogenic state is if you keep track of your macros. What are macros? Macros, or macronutrients, are essentially the three major nutrients that make up your diet: fat, protein, and carbohydrates. When you are able to track your macros in an attentive manner, then you have more control over your diet. Also, it would make it easier for you to get the results that you want.

Get Yourself a Diet Buddy

The human spirit is resilient. One should never be so quick to underestimate the power of human perseverance. However, there are still limits to a human being's capacity. It's encouraged for you to always be confident with anything that you do in life. But if there is an opportunity for you to share your burdens with someone else, then you should make the most out of it. After all, the cliché still rings true: two heads are better than one. When you have a diet buddy, you have someone who can help keep you honest. Also, you are accountable to someone. And this is going to help you stick to your diet.

Prepare Yourself for Keto Flu

The keto flu isn't a real flu. However, there are a lot of people who might experience flu-like symptoms after starting a keto diet. While there are no conclusive findings as to why this is the case, it's often attributed to the drastic change in lifestyle and diet. In order for you to not get overwhelmed by the flu, it's best that you just expect it and prepare for it. Consider it a minor setback as you embark on your journey to optimal health and wellness. After all, these symptoms don't really last in the long term.

Engage in Meal Planning and Prepping

One of the most challenging aspects of dieting is trying to figure out where your next meal will come from. Consider the possibility that you are at the office and a bunch of your friends invite you out to dinner after work. Of course, you become hesitant because you know that you're on a diet. However, you don't want to deprive yourself of social indulgences. In these situations, it would be really handy if you just had packed meals that you had prepared beforehand. That way, you can still go out with your friends and you wouldn't have to worry about having to cheat on your diet.

Don't Give Up Right Away

Patience is key when it comes to health and dieting. You could be trying your absolute hardest and the results still might not come when you want them to. During these times, it can be very easy to feel discouraged, and that discouragement could eventually lead to you quitting. However, you shouldn't allow that to happen to you. It's important that you stay persistent and resilient as you try to better yourself through food. Just trust in the process and believe that if you stay consistent, the desired results are going to come eventually.

Focus on the Positive

Always focus on the positive. Instead of thinking about how much it sucks for you to be dieting, try to focus on all that you stand to gain from staying disciplined. Sure, there are plenty of people out there who are enjoying their lives without limits. However, they also have to deal with the consequences of their actions. While it may not feel like it right now, you are doing a good thing, and your future self is going to look back on your present self and thank you for choosing to stay committed.

Keto Mexican Rice: The Ultimate Keto Substitute for Rice

Perhaps the best thing about this keto Mexican rice recipe is the fact that it's so easy to make. Never mind just how healthy this dish is. When you're craving something filling and delicious, but you don't have much time (or culinary skills) at your disposal, then this is a great recipe for you. For a lot of cultures, rice is a staple in every meal. However, rice can be dangerous to one's weight loss goals because of how calorically dense it is. That's why this keto Mexican rice is such a lifesaver for rice lovers who are on the keto diet.

The base for the 'rice' in this recipe is cauliflower. As hard as it might be to imagine, there is a way of cooking cauliflower to make it resemble real rice. And the good thing about cauliflower is that it is really low in calories and it can be very filling. If you're looking to limit your carb count and lower your glucose levels, then this recipe should be a staple in your cookbook. Seasoned with loads of

Mexican spices, it would be hard to grow bored of a dish that is packed with flavor.

Number of Servings: 6 servings

Preparation Time: 5 minutes

Cooking Time: 20 minutes

Macros per Serving:

- Fat: 22 g
- Protein: 29 g
- Carbohydrates: 7 g

Total Calories per Serving: 352 kcal

Ingredients:

- 1 lb. ground beef
- ¼ medium onion, diced
- ½ red pepper, diced
- 1 cup diced tomatoes
- 12 oz. cauliflower rice
- 3 tbsp. Mexican taco seasoning
- ½ cup chicken broth
- 1 ½ cups cheddar cheese

Directions:

For the Cauliflower Rice:

1. To make the cauliflower rice, take the cauliflower heads and remove the stems.
2. Make sure to wash the heads thoroughly to ensure that they are free of any dirt or pests.
3. Chop the cauliflower heads up into multiple smaller florets.
4. Place the florets into a food processor or powerful blender.
5. Dice the florets into small bits or until it achieves the consistency and size of grains of rice.

For the Keto Mexican Rice:

1. Prepare a large skillet and place it over medium heat.
2. Place the ground beef into the skillet and cook until it browns. Add the onions and peppers. Continue to cook the beef until it has completely browned and there are no pink spots.
3. Stir the taco seasoning into the beef mixture and spread evenly.
4. Add the tomatoes and cauliflower rice to the skillet. Continue to stir thoroughly to make sure that all ingredients are properly distributed.
5. Add the broth into the skillet and bring to a simmer. Once simmering, reduce the heat to medium-low heat and cook until the

cauliflower rice softens to the desired consistency.

6. Sprinkle the cheese over the rice and cover. Allow the cheese to melt.

7. Serve on a large plate and garnish with avocado, cream cheese, sour cream, and/or cilantro.

Enjoy!

Keto Tater Tots: Cheesy Bursts of Delight

Once in a while, you might get a craving for tater tots out of the blue. Unfortunately, the tater tot in its traditional form is a big no-no while on the keto diet. Traditionally, tater tots are made from potatoes, but potatoes pack way too much starch and too many carbs for them to be permissible under the keto philosophy of eating. On top of potatoes, traditional tater tots also make use of breadcrumbs for the coating. That's way too many carbs and we all know that carbs are the enemy in a keto diet. However, there's just something so comforting (and maybe even nostalgic) about tater tots. That's why it's so hard for a lot of people to just let them go altogether.

Fortunately, there is a keto alternative to this old favorite. This recipe is going to allow practitioners of the keto diet an opportunity to still eat this familiar and nostalgic dish. The potatoes are replaced by cauliflower and you won't even need to make use of breadcrumbs to achieve the traditional tater tot consistency. With these key replacements, it's still possible to enjoy the comfort of tater tots without having to sacrifice ketosis. They're also incredibly easy to make as well.

Number of Servings: 8 servings

Preparation Time: 5 minutes

Cooking Time: 15 minutes

Macros per Serving:

- Fat: 11 g
- Protein: 7 g
- Carbohydrates: 4 g

Total Calories per Serving: 142 kcal

Ingredients:

- 1 ½ lb. cauliflower rice
- ¼ cup avocado oil
- 1 large egg
- 1 ½ cup mozzarella cheese
- 2 cloves minced garlic
- ¾ tsp sea salt

Directions:

1. Prepare a large sauté pan or wok and place over medium-high heat. Stir cauliflower rice and oil into the pan and cook until lightly

brown. Make sure no moisture is left in the pan.

2. While the cauliflower is cooking, whisk the egg in a bowl.

3. Add mozzarella, garlic, and sea salt to the egg wash.

4. When the cauliflower is finished cooking, stir immediately into the bowl along with the egg. The heat of the cauliflower rice should be enough to melt the mozzarella and develop a sticky consistency.

5. Mix everything thoroughly and then divide everything up into small cauliflower rice balls. These will serve as the tots.

6. Flatten the tater tots slightly to make sure that they will cook thoroughly and properly.

7. Take the large pan and wipe it clean. Make sure that no moisture or cauliflower rice pieces are left behind.

8. Place the pan back on medium heat and add a thin layer of olive oil or nonstick spray. Lay down as many tater tots as you can in a single layer. Make sure that none of them come into contact with one another while cooking.

9. Fry the tots for around 2 minutes and then flip. Cook the other side for another 2 minutes or until it has achieved your desired texture.

10. Add more oil as necessary until you've finished cooking all the tater tots.

Enjoy!

Keto Beef Taco: Low in Carbs and High in Flavor

With just 7 grams of carbohydrates in every serving, you know that you can enjoy the guilt-free experience of eating these amazing tacos. If you're allergic to gluten or if you're trying to avoid it altogether, then you will be happy to know that this recipe is gluten-free as well. There's nothing quite like being able to indulge in the crunch of a taco shell once you get a craving for Mexican food. There is a reason why so many Mexican restaurants and food trucks are a go-to for people who get sudden cravings throughout various points of the day. But again, there is a catch. A lot of these tacos from these Mexican restaurants (most of them fast-food joints) aren't too healthy for the belly.

Fortunately, this recipe is a subtle reinvention of the taco as we know it. It's going to be able to hit that spot and scratch that itch for Mexican comfort food without you feeling like punishing yourself with a 10-mile run right after eating it. It's completely guilt-free, but it still packs a punch that is sure to tingle your taste buds. Also, part of what makes fast-food joints so appealing is the fact that they're so convenient. Well, you have no excuse because this recipe is as simple and as convenient as can be. You won't need any high-grade culinary skills to pull this dish off. To lessen the cooking and preparation time, try to prepare your taco shells in large numbers in advance. That way, whenever you start craving tacos, all you have to prepare is the meat and the fillings.

Number of Servings: 6 servings

Preparation Time: 15 minutes

Cooking Time: 10 minutes

Macros per Serving:

- Fat: 33 g
- Protein: 28 g
- Carbohydrates: 7 g

Total Calories per Serving: 432 kcal

Ingredients:

For the taco shells:

- 9 oz. shredded cheddar cheese

For the taco meat:

- 1 lb. lean ground beef

- 1 pack low-carb Mexican seasoning
- 2 tbsp. tomato paste
- ½ cup beef broth
- Salt and pepper to taste

Toppings (optional)

- 2 cups chopped lettuce
- ½ cup salsa
- ½ cup sour cream
- 1 medium avocado, sliced
- ½ cup shredded cheese
- ¼ cup minced purple onion
- ¼ cup chopped cilantro

Directions:

For the taco shells:

1. Preheat the oven to 375 degrees F or 190 degrees C.
2. Situate one rack in the upper third of the oven. Situate another rack in the lower third of the oven. Prepare two large sheet pans with parchment paper. Draw three 6-inch circles on each sheet of parchment.
3. Take the shredded cheese and spread it out evenly in large circles. Lay it out in as flatly a manner as you can.
4. Bake the cheese on the upper and lower partitions for 5 minutes. After 5 minutes,

switch the places of the baking sheets. Bake for another 5-10 minutes or until tiny holes have appeared on the surface of the cheese circles.

5. Remove the cheese from the oven and allow to cool for a bit. While cooling, make use of spatulas or rounded spoons to shape the cheese into taco shells.

6. Allow to cool completely and store in a refrigerator to preserve freshness and crunch.

For the filling:

1. To prepare, chop up the lettuce and cilantro. Make sure that they are washed and cleaned.

2. Slice the avocados.

3. Mince the onion.

4. Prepare sour cream, salsa, and cheese in individual bowls.

5. Prepare a pan and put over medium heat. Crumble the ground beef into the pan and stir thoroughly with a spatula.

6. Once the beef has begun to brown, add the tomato paste and stir. After that, add the beef broth and bring to a simmer. Allow the meat to fully absorb the liquid. Add the Mexican seasoning together with salt and pepper to taste.

7. Divide the taco meat evenly among the six shells.
8. Add the toppings according to your personal preference.

Enjoy!

Pimiento Cheese Meatballs:

Cheese and Meat in a Fun Form

Regardless of how old you are or what your cultural background might be, meatballs are likely going to be an old favorite. These spheres of protein and fat are commonplace on many dinner tables all across the world. Part of the reason why they're so popular is that they come in such a fun and unique form. Also, they're incredibly versatile. Meatballs can be made from pork, beef, fish, and poultry. Sometimes, there are even fusions of various meats that are made into meatballs. It's no wonder why this dish in particular, resonates with so many people. It's versatile enough to cater to a variety of different tastes and preferences.

However, meatballs in their traditional form are often made with lots of breadcrumbs in order to keep the meat together in ball form. And as you may already know, breadcrumbs are a big no-no in the world of keto. That's why this recipe is going to offer you a unique take on the meatball; one that does not require the use of breadcrumbs. However, if you're looking to add these meatballs to your spaghetti, it might end up being counterintuitive. In any case, these meatballs are so tasty that you're probably going to be happy eating them on their own. You can also have them with keto-friendly sides, such as cauliflower mash, broccoli and cheese, creamed green cabbage, and more.

This meatball recipe in particular is also going to be a welcome culinary experience for cheese-lovers. Paired with the spicy taste of pimiento, this is a meatball recipe that is unlike any other.

Number of Servings: 4 servings

Preparation Time: 10 minutes

Cooking Time: 40 minutes

Macros per Serving:

- Fat: 52 g
- Protein: 41 g

- Carbohydrates: 1 g

Total Calories per Serving: 651 kcal

Ingredients:

For the pimiento cheese:

- ⅓ cup of mayonnaise
- 4 oz. of grated cheddar cheese
- ¼ cup pimiento or pickled jalapenos
- 1 tbsp. Dijon mustard
- 1 tsp paprika powder
- Cayenne pepper to taste

For the meatballs:

- 1 ½ lbs. ground beef
- 1 large egg
- Salt and pepper to taste

Directions:

1. Preheat the oven to 400 degrees F or 200 degrees C.
2. Take all of the ingredients for the pimiento cheese and place them into a large bowl. Make sure that all of these ingredients are mixed together thoroughly.
3. Add the ground beef and the egg to the cheese mixture. Thoroughly combine all of

the ingredients together. Add salt and pepper to taste.

4. Using your hands, form the contents of the bowl into equal sized balls.

5. On a large baking tray, arrange meatballs in neat rows. Make sure that the balls don't come in contact with one another.

6. Bake meatballs for around 30 to 40 minutes or until the surface of the balls begin to char.

Enjoy!

Keto Pizza: Indulge in a Slice of Keto Goodness

Who doesn't love pizza? It's probably one of the best comfort foods there is. When you're trying to get your picky six-year-old to eat their dinner, you bribe them with pizza. When you're in a rush on your lunch break and you only have an hour to get a bite to eat, a slice of pizza always hit the spot. And, one of the great things about pizza is that it's incredibly versatile. There are different types of pizza that can hit the spot for just about anyone. But all of the carbs that you find in a traditional slice of pizza make it non-viable for practitioners of the keto diet. Fortunately, there are recipes like this that are designed to fill that pizza-shaped hole in your heart.

With this recipe, you can have the entire pizza ready to eat in about 20 minutes. You also don't have to spend too much time poring over the dish either. You don't have to be a renowned Italian chef for the dish to taste great. At the end of the day, you need to spare time for the good things in life. And make no mistake about it. The time that you set aside to make this pizza is definitely worth it. This would make for a great dish to serve at parties or gatherings with friends and family. And the absolute best part of this recipe is that you're only getting 5 grams of carbs per slice.

Number of Servings: 8 servings

Preparation Time: 5 minutes

Cooking Time: 15 minutes

Macros per Serving:

- Fat: 19 g
- Protein: 14 g
- Carbohydrates: 5 g

Total Calories per Serving: 249 kcal

Ingredients:

For the crust:

- 2 cups shredded mozzarella cheese
- 1 oz. cream cheese
- 1 cup almond flour
- 1 egg
- 1 tsp of baking powder
- Italian seasoning to taste
- Garlic powder to taste

For the toppings (to your preference):

- Cheese (mozzarella, parmesan, feta, etc.)
- Meats/protein (beef, pepperoni, turkey, chicken, etc.)
- Vegetables (onion, pepper, spinach, olives, jalapeño, etc.)
- Sugar-free tomato sauce

Directions:

1. Preheat the oven to 450 degrees F or 230 degrees C.
2. Add the mozzarella and cream cheese into a large microwavable bowl. Microwave the cheeses for 45 seconds.
3. Remove the bowl from the microwave and immediately add the egg, baking powder, Italian seasoning, and garlic powder.
4. Mix all of the contents of the bowl thoroughly until everything is well-

incorporated. This will serve as the dough of the pizza.

5. Transfer the dough onto a large piece of parchment paper and then cover it with another piece of parchment paper. Take a rolling pin and flatten it out until it becomes ¼ of an inch thick. Remove the parchment paper and fix the shape if desired.

6. Transfer the pizza onto a baking sheet lined with parchment paper and bake for 10 minutes or until the cheese starts to harden.

7. Remove the pizza crust from the oven and then add all of your desired toppings such as tomato sauce, cheese, meat, etc.

8. Bake the pizza for 5-8 minutes more or until the cheese begins to bubble.

Enjoy!

Keto Peanut Butter Cookies: Tiny Bites of Peanut Butter Heaven

One of the biggest disappointments that people have when they start the keto diet is that desserts are practically a no-go. Say goodbye to all of those Snickers bars that you used to indulge in during your breaks at the office. You don't have the luxury of having a slice of cake after dinner anymore. Those delicious apple pies that catch your attention every time you pass the bakery are something that you can't eat on your diet. It's frustrating to know that there's all of this deliciousness out there that you can't have because you've decided to be fitter and healthier.

However, you're looking at it all wrong. Just because you're on a diet doesn't mean that you can't indulge in deliciousness anymore. You just have to be able to go about it right, and this is the kind of recipe that can do exactly that. Everyone loves cookies. You should never trust anyone who doesn't enjoy a good old cookie every once in a while. And if you get a hankering for a cookie, you don't have to deprive yourself in those moments. Ketosis doesn't have to be compromised when enjoying a cookie, so follow this recipe and reward yourself with a dessert. This cookie recipe in particular is especially appealing to people who are fans of peanut butter.

Number of Servings: 12 servings

Preparation Time: 10 minutes

Cooking Time: 15 minutes

Macros per Serving:

- Fat: 11 g
- Protein: 6 g
- Carbohydrates: 12.5 g

Total Calories per Serving: 133 kcal

Ingredients:

- 1 cup peanut butter
- 1 large egg
- 1 tsp sugar-free vanilla extract
- ½ cup low-calorie natural sweetener

Directions:

1. Preheat oven to 350 degrees F or 175 degrees C. Prepare a baking sheet and line it with parchment paper.
2. Combine the peanut butter, egg, vanilla extract, and sweetener into a large bowl. Mix all of the ingredients thoroughly until the desired consistency of the dough is achieved.
3. Roll the dough into 12 balls of equal sizes. Place the balls on a baking sheet and press them down with a fork in a crisscross fashion.
4. Bake the cookies in the preheated oven until the edges brown. This should take roughly around 12 to 15 minutes. Allow the cookies to cool on a baking sheet for one minute.
5. Transfer the cookies to a wire rack and allow to cool completely.

Enjoy!

Chicken Zucchini Pasta: Carbo Loading Without the Carbs

There is almost an infinite amount of pasta recipes that pop up in cookbooks, on internet sites, cooking shows, podcasts, and all that jazz. And it can be very difficult for any one of these recipes to set themselves apart from the others. In fact, it's likely that you have a stereotypical concept of a pasta recipe in your mind right now. It's a nicely constructed bowl of pasta that's sprinkled with lots of herbs and a few slices of perfectly grilled chicken. Well, this recipe is going to add to that old cliché. However, there is a twist. This recipe is keto-friendly.

Instead of using pasta in the traditional sense, this recipe is going to make use of zucchini. This means that you get to indulge in your pasta cravings without having to worry about feeling bloated. You also won't have to worry about those carb-crashes that you get after eating a huge plate of regular pasta. This recipe is proof that with a little ingenuity and creativity, you can have fun with your diet. It's all just a matter of thinking outside of the box and showing a willingness to try new things.

This keto pasta recipe in particular is going to be packed with flavor. With a creamy garlic base and shrimp as a protein, it would be hard to resist having multiple servings of this dish.

Number of Servings: 5 servings

Preparation Time: 10 minutes

Cooking Time: 15 minutes

Macros per Serving:

- Fat: 30 g
- Protein: 35 g
- Carbohydrates: 3 g

Total Calories per Serving: 389 kcal

Ingredients:

- 2 lbs. zucchini noodles
- ¼ tsp kosher salt
- 1 tbsp. olive oil
- 1 lb. peeled and deveined shrimp
- 1 tbsp. minced garlic
- 2 tbsp. butter

- 4 oz. cream cheese
- ½ cup heavy cream
- ½ cup Parmesan cheese
- ¼ tsp red pepper flakes
- Salt and pepper to taste

Directions:

1. Take a sheet pan and line it with paper towels.
2. Place all of the zucchini noodles on the paper towel and season with salt.
3. Allow the zucchini to sit for around 30 minutes to drain out excess water.
4. Prepare a skillet and place it over medium-high heat.
5. Add olive oil, shrimp, and garlic into the skillet. Cook the shrimp until it becomes pink on both sides.
6. Add the butter into the skillet and bring the heat down to medium. Let the butter melt and then add the cream cheese, parmesan cheese, red pepper flakes, and heavy cream.
7. Season with salt and pepper to taste.
8. Stir the cheese mixture continuously until all of the cheese has melted.
9. Add shrimp and zucchini noodles to the pan and stir thoroughly.
10. Cook for around 3 to 4 minutes or until the zucchini softens.

Enjoy!

Shrimp and Grits: Delicious Cauliflower Grit and Grind

For this recipe, cauliflower is going to make a reappearance. As we have seen, cauliflower is a powerful ingredient in the keto world. There are so many things that you can do with it. And the best part is that it's incredibly low in carbohydrates and calories. This means that you can indulge in it as much as you want without having to worry about packing on those extra pounds. It's a great replacement for rice, bread, pasta, and all of those carb-heavy food items that would normally keep you from achieving ketosis.

But of course, the cauliflower isn't going to be the star of this meal. We have reserved that position for shrimps with a side of arugula for extra flavor. Unless you're allergic, it's very likely that you are a fan of shrimp as they offer a unique gastronomic experience. They are unlike most other proteins that you would typically consume on a daily basis. Also, they are relatively easy to procure and they aren't as expensive as other high-end seafood like lobster.

This recipe is going to call for some very light seasoning and cooking to really allow the natural flavors of the shrimp to shine. The shrimp will be spiced up just a little bit to make it a little more interesting. The arugula and cauliflower are there to add a little more texture and complexity to the meal. All in all, the different flavor profiles of these ingredients can make for a very interesting dining experience.

Number of Servings: 4 servings

Preparation Time: 5 minutes

Cooking Time: 20 minutes

Macros per Serving:

- Fat: 15 g
- Protein: 24 g
- Carbohydrates: 12 g

Total Calories per Serving: 273 kcal

Ingredients:

- 1 lb. peeled and deveined shrimp
- 4 cups cauliflower rice
- 4 cups baby arugula
- 1 cup whole milk
- 3 sliced garlic cloves
- 1 tbsp. butter

- ½ cup goat cheese
- 2 tsp garlic powder
- 1 tbsp. paprika
- ½ tsp cayenne pepper
- 2 tbsp. olive oil
- Salt and pepper to taste

Directions:

1. Place the peeled shrimp into a large Ziploc plastic bag.
2. In a small bowl, add in the paprika, cayenne pepper, and garlic powder. Combine all three spices thoroughly. Add in the spice mix into the bag of shrimp. Seal the plastic bag and shake to make sure that the shrimps are coated properly. Place the plastic bag into the fridge.
3. Prepare a medium-sized pot and place over medium heat. Add butter and allow to melt. Then, add the cauliflower rice and cook until it releases moisture. This should take 2 to 3 minutes.
4. Pour in half of the milk and bring to a simmer. Allow to simmer for around 6 to 8 minutes as the cauliflower gradually absorbs the milk.
5. Add the remaining milk and allow to simmer for 10 minutes or until the liquid achieves a thick and creamy consistency.

Stir in the goat cheese and add salt and pepper to taste.

6. In a large skillet, heat the olive oil over medium heat. Add the garlic cloves and cook until fragrant. Add the arugula and cook until the leaves start to wilt. This should take around 3 to 4 minutes.

7. Add salt and pepper to taste.

8. Remove the bag of shrimps from the refrigerator and add it to the arugula. Cook and sauté the shrimp for an additional 3 minutes. Season with salt and pepper.

9. To plate, use the grits as the base of the serving dish. Gradually add the shrimp and arugula on top of the bed of cauliflower grits.

Enjoy!

Chicken Salad Stuffed in Bell Peppers: An Explosion of Flavor

This fun and colorful dish can make for a great snack or even a full-on meal. It might not be something that you find yourself eating on a daily basis. However, it's a really unique dish that can help add some vibrancy and excitement to your meal plan. In fact, you might love it so much to the point that you eventually add it to your daily menu. This chicken salad is made with a base of

Greek yogurt so that it stays keto friendly. But everyone knows that chicken salad can be really bland. That's why this recipe serves it in bell peppers to make things a little more flavorful and exciting.

This chicken salad is going to offer you a nice and creamy flavor with just a bit of tanginess to it. If you choose to cook it in large batches, you can simply grab some salad from the fridge for whenever you need a quick snack or when you're not sure what to pack for lunch. It's always a nice and healthy way to keep yourself full and emotionally satisfied. The chicken salad in itself is already amazing. The fact that it's served in a bell pepper is just a bonus. With this recipe, you won't have to do any actual cooking. You can just buy all of the ingredients that are readily available at the store and just combine them when you get home. For the chicken, you can purchase a whole rotisserie chicken from wherever is convenient.

Number of Servings: 6 servings

Preparation Time: 5 minutes

Cooking Time: 0 minutes

Macros per Serving:

- Fat: 3 g

- Protein: 7 g
- Carbohydrates: 16 g

Total Calories per Serving: 116 kcal

Ingredients:

- ⅔ cup Greek yogurt
- 2 tbsp. Dijon mustard
- 2 tbsp. seasoned rice vinegar
- Cubed chicken meat from rotisserie chicken
- ⅓ cup fresh parsley
- 4 stalks sliced celery
- 1 bunch sliced scallions
- 1 pint quartered cherry tomatoes
- ½ cucumber
- 3 bell peppers, halved and deseeded
- Salt and pepper to taste

Directions:

1. In a medium-sized bowl, mix the Greek yogurt, rice vinegar, and mustard. Whisk thoroughly until all ingredients are well-combined. Add parsley and season with salt and pepper.
2. Add the chicken, celery, scallions, tomatoes, and cucumber. Combine well.
3. Spoon the chicken salad into the deseeded bell peppers.
4. Top with scallions for garnish.

Enjoy!

Keto French Toast

There's really not much to say about this recipe other than the fact that it's french toast in keto form. French toast is a comforting and indulgent food that is typically consumed for breakfast. However, there should be nothing that stops you from having it throughout various points of the day. In order to enjoy this french toast without feeling guilty about it, you should opt for a paleo or keto-friendly bread that is low in carbs. Ideally, this bread would be made out of almond flour or coconut flour.

With regard to the toppings, there are a variety of keto-friendly options at your disposal. The recipe itself suggests the use of a yogurt-based topping. However, you don't have to limit yourself to that. You can make use of berries if you want to add something sweet on your toast. But, you can also add some textural elements like shredded coconut and nuts. To sweeten your French toast, you can make use of keto-friendly items like stevia. Cinnamon powder is also a very popular option.

Number of Servings: 2 servings

Preparation Time: 5 minutes

Cooking Time: 15 minutes

Macros per Serving:

- Fat: 58 g
- Protein: 29 g
- Carbohydrates: 17 g

Total Calories per Serving: 683 kcal

Ingredients:

- 1 loaf keto-friendly or paleo-friendly bread (made out of almond or coconut flour)
- 1 tbsp. butter
- ⅓ cup coconut yogurt
- 2 tsp stevia
- 1 tsp vanilla extract
- Optional garnishes or toppings: shredded coconut, cacao nibs, berries, nuts, etc.

Directions:

1. Prepare the paleo bread loaf by slicing it into three equal pieces. After that, cut each corresponding slice in half, lengthwise. You should now have six slices of bread.
2. Prepare a large frying pan and place it over medium heat. Add butter to the pan and swirl.

3. Once the pan is hot, place two slices of bread into the pan and cook on both sides until they all reach a golden-brown color.
4. While waiting for the toasting process to finish, prepare a medium-sized bowl for the yogurt topping.
5. Add coconut yogurt, vanilla, and stevia to the bowl. Whisk the yogurt until it starts to thicken. If you want your yogurt to be a little sweeter, add stevia and vanilla extract to taste.
6. To plate, place the toasted sticks of bread on the base of the plate. Top it off with the yogurt mixture and additional toppings.

Enjoy!

Chicken and Waffles: Good for the Keto's Soul

When talking about traditional soul food, it can be very hard to have a discussion that doesn't involve chicken and waffles somehow. To the uninitiated, chicken and waffles can seem like an odd pairing. However, there are a lot of things going on for this dish that just work. Take the savory and comforting flavor of fried chicken that we are all familiar with and pair it with the sweet, crunchy, and fluffy flavor of the waffle. It's a match that shouldn't work, but it does. In fact, the chicken and waffle dish has a huge cult following. But again, you probably know where we're going with this: it's not keto.

First off, the breading on the skin of the chicken is incredibly high in carbohydrates. And the waffles in themselves are carb-packed pockets of goodness. However, there is a way to get around this. With this keto recipe, you can still enjoy the comfort of this traditional soul food without getting out of a state of ketosis. With a few key adjustments and alternatives, you can still recreate this classic dish that is sure to warm your heart and fill your belly. Not only does this dish look amazing on a plate, it's going to taste like nothing you've ever had in your life.

Number of Servings: 4 servings

Preparation Time: 5 minutes

Cooking Time: 20 minutes

Macros per Serving:

- Fat: 32 g
- Protein: 34 g
- Carbohydrates: 5 g

Total Calories per Serving: 453 kcal

Ingredients:

For the waffles:

- 2 tbsp. melted butter
- 3 large eggs with yolks and whites separated
- ¼ cup milk
- 1 cup almond flour
- ½ tsp salt
- 1 tsp vanilla
- 1 tsp erythritol

For the chicken:

- 1 cup buttermilk

- 2 medium-sized chicken breast fillets
- 1 large egg
- ⅓ cup almond flour
- Coconut oil for frying
- 1 tsp paprika
- ¼ tsp cayenne pepper
- Salt and pepper to taste

Directions:

1. Cut the chicken up into halves in a lengthwise fashion. And then, cut the sliced pieces in half in a lengthwise fashion as well. You should now have four strips of chicken breasts. Soak the chicken in buttermilk overnight.
2. Take the chicken out of the buttermilk and then season it with salt, pepper, paprika, and cayenne pepper.
3. In a large bowl, beat a large egg and then set it aside. In a separate bowl, mix almond flour together with salt and pepper. Take every strip of the chicken and coat it with egg wash. And then, coat it with the almond flour. Repeat the process so that there are two layers of flour.
4. Prepare a large skillet and heat some olive oil on it. Once the oil is hot, quickly cook both sides of the chicken strip until the outside layer begins to brown. Then, place

each chicken strip on a baking sheet and cover it with a layer of foil. Bake the chicken at 350 degrees F or 170 degrees C for 15 minutes.

5. While the chicken is cooking, preheat your waffle maker. In a large bowl, whisk the egg yolk, milk, melted butter, erythritol, and vanilla extract together.

6. In a separate bowl, beat the egg whites with a mixer until they form stiff peaks. Then, you should carefully fold the egg into the batter, adding one half at a time.

7. Coat or spray the waffle maker with oil or butter, and then add ⅓ cup of the batter and cook each waffle for around 6 minutes.

8. To serve, place the waffles on the base of the plate. Top each waffle with the chicken. Add your desired toppings such as bacon, pickles, and keto-friendly sauces.

Enjoy!

Spicy Curry Cauliflower Soup: Heartwarming and Filling

There's just no beating around the bush with this particular dish. It's really tasty! There's a certain nutty and buttery taste that comes about when you properly roast cauliflower. It's very mild but it's also incredibly distinct. But the real kicker here comes from the curry paste. It's just spicy enough to make the dish interesting, but it won't be too spicy to the point that it overpowers all the other flavors of the dish. The mildness of the cauliflower is designed to blend in well with the power of the curry. However, there is another layer to that flavor as well. The coconut milk offers the curry dish a creamy and rich flavor that will leave you wanting more after every bite.

When you first taste this soup, it will be hard for you to believe that it's healthy. Due to the richness of the flavor, you would automatically think that this dish is packed with a lot of unnecessary calories. However, you will be happy to know that a single bowl of this cauliflower soup offers only 225 calories and 14 grams of carbohydrates.

With regard to the curry paste, you can always opt to make your own from scratch. However, in order to save yourself time, it might be best for you to just buy ready-to-use curry paste from the store. And for the coconut milk, it would be best for you to get the full-fat variant from a can. The creaminess and thickness of full-fat coconut milk is what would really serve this recipe best.

Number of Servings: 6 servings

Preparation Time: 10 minutes

Cooking Time: 30 minutes

Macros per Serving:

- Fat: 18 g
- Protein: 4 g
- Carbohydrates: 14 g

Total Calories per Serving: 224 kcal

Ingredients:

- 1 large cauliflower head
- 1 tbsp. olive oil
- 4 oz. Thai red curry paste
- 1 medium-sized onion

- 4 cups vegetable broth
- 14 oz. can of unsweetened coconut milk
- ¼ tsp salt
- 1 tbsp. lemon juice
- Sliced scallions for garnish

Directions:

1. Preheat the oven to 400 degrees F or 205 degrees C.
2. Remove the florets from the cauliflower head. Quarter the onion.
3. Lay the cauliflower florets and the onion slices on a baking tray lined with parchment paper. Toss with olive oil and bake for 20 minutes.
4. Prepare a high-power blender or food processor and add the cauliflower and onions. Add vegetable broth to the blender and pulse until you achieve a smooth and creamy consistency.
5. Pour the puree from the blender into a pot and place it over medium heat. Add the coconut milk, salt, lemon juice, and curry paste. Stir the mixture thoroughly until all ingredients have combined together.
6. Cook until the soup is hot all the way through. Serve with sliced scallions as garnish.

Enjoy!

Keto Pretzels: A Common Street-Food Favorite in Keto Form

This keto pretzel recipe might not seem all that inviting just by its name alone, but it definitely packs a lot of flavor. When you think of pretzels, you may think of a plain twisted mound of dough that's fried or baked. You would typically consume it with some kind of topping like cream cheese or cinnamon powder. While a pretzel can be a convenient and comforting go-to for a lot of people who are just looking to munch on something, it can be so much more than that.

First of all, being that pretzels are essentially twisted bread, they're not keto-friendly. However, this recipe is going to reinvent the pretzel by making use of keto-friendly ingredients. On top of that, these pretzels are going to be infused with lots of delicious cheese. With almond flour as a base, you are also going to be treated to a very unique and distinct texture that regular flour would never be able to replicate.

Oh, and did we mention that cheese was involved?

Number of Servings: 8 servings

Preparation Time: 15 minutes

Cooking Time: 15 minutes

Macros per Serving:

- Fat: 24 g
- Protein: 18 g
- Carbohydrates: 8 g

Total Calories per Serving: 315 kcal

Ingredients:

- 3 cups shredded mozzarella cheese
- 3 medium-sized eggs
- 2 oz. cream cheese
- 2 cups almond flour
- 1 tbsp. baking powder
- 1 tbsp. salt

Directions:

1. Preheat the oven to 400 degrees F or 205 degrees C.
2. Prepare a baking sheet lined with parchment paper.

3. In a medium-sized bowl, pour in the baking powder and almond flour. Whisk these ingredients thoroughly and set aside.

4. In a large microwave-safe bowl, mix the cream cheese and mozzarella. Situate the cream cheese at the bottom of the bowl with the mozzarella directly on top of it. This is because you want the mozzarella to get most of the exposure to the heat of the microwave.

5. Melt the cheese inside the microwave for around 30 seconds. Take the bowl out of the microwave and stir. Return the bowl to the microwave and heat for another 30 seconds. Repeat this process over and over again until the cheese has achieved a smooth and creamy consistency. Be very careful not to cook all of the cheese in one go because you would risk of burning it.

6. The cheese melting process should take around 2 minutes or so. Once the cheese has completely melted, transfer the cheese to a food processor. Add the flour mixture along with two eggs. Pulse the contents of the processor at high speed until you achieve a dough-like consistency. Expect the dough to feel sticky.

7. Wrap a pastry board with plastic wrap and ensure tautness of the wrap. To make sure

that the board doesn't slip and slide, wrap the bottom parts of it as well. The plastic wrap serves as a measure to keep the dough from sticking to the board.

8. Approximate the dough into 8 equal parts and divide them accordingly. Roll the dough into ropes that are around an inch thick.

9. Slice the dough with a knife into ¾ inch pieces. If done correctly, you should end up with 70 to 75 pretzel bites. Place the bites onto the baking sheet that was prepared earlier on.

10. Place the remaining egg into a bowl and whisk. This will serve as a wash for the pretzels. Brush the surface of the pretzels with the egg wash and season with salt according to taste.

11. Bake the pretzels for approximately 12 minutes or until they achieve a light golden-brown color on the outside. After that, broil the pretzels for another 2 minutes to make the surfaces crunchy and crisp. However, be very careful not to burn your pretzels during the broiling process.

12. Remove from oven and allow to cool before serving.

Enjoy!

Keto Pot Pie: A Modern Keto Twist on a Classic Dish

Eating low-carb doesn't only encourage you to feel better about yourself. It also forces you to pay close attention to the food that you're eating. As a result, it's more likely that you would enjoy the meals that you prepare a lot more. When you devote more time and attention into preparing the food that you eat, the more likely it would be for the food to taste better. The classic chicken pot pie is a dish that hasn't really been reimagined in dramatic fashion since its inception. However, with the recent rise of the keto diet, there are various recipes that exist out there that provide a keto-friendly version of this dish.

Without violating your body's ability to enter a state of ketosis, this low-carb chicken pot pie recipe has a flaky biscuit as a crust which resembles the real thing. Also, the filling of the pie is creamy and garlicky. This means that you're still getting that full flavor that you've grown to love from traditional chicken pot pie recipes. There are going to be some carrots and peas integrated into this recipe. However, they will not carry enough carbohydrates for you to be concerned. But if you aren't comfortable with eating these food items, the recipe still works without them. It's still important to note that each serving carries only 6 grams of carbohydrates.

Number of Servings: 8 servings

Preparation Time: 10 minutes

Cooking Time: 15 minutes

Macros per Serving:

- Fat: 11 g
- Protein: 24 g
- Carbohydrates: 6 g

Total Calories per Serving: 219 kcal

Ingredients:

For the chicken filling:

- 1 ½ lbs. of cubed chicken breasts
- 4 oz. finely chopped yellow onions
- ¼ cup finely diced carrots
- ¼ cup fresh green peas
- 1 tbsp. butter
- 1 clove crushed garlic
- ½ tsp dried thyme
- 1 tbsp. white wine vinegar

- 1 cup low-sodium chicken broth
- ½ cup heavy cream
- Salt and pepper to taste

For the topping:

- 1 cup fine almond flour
- 1 tbsp. ground flaxseed
- ½ tsp xanthan gum
- ¼ tsp salt
- 1 tsp of baking powder
- 2 tbsp. sour cream
- 2 tbsp. butter
- 1 egg white

Directions:

1. Preheat the oven to 400 degrees F or 205 degrees C.
2. Grease a round 9" baking pan.

For the chicken filling:

1. Prepare a large skillet and place it over medium-high heat. Melt the butter in the skillet.
2. When the butter is completely melted, add the diced chicken to the pan and cook. Stir the chicken occasionally until it browns on all sides. However, you don't have to cook it all the way through yet.

3. Add the onions and carrots to the skillet. Season the contents of the skillet with salt and pepper. Turn the heat down to medium low. Cook the contents of the skillet and stir occasionally until the onions begin to brown and caramelize. Stir in the garlic and thyme. Cook for another minute.
4. Stir the vinegar into the mixture and wait for it to substantially evaporate.
5. Turn the heat up to medium high and allow the broth to simmer. Stir every so often. After around 15-20 minutes, the broth should thicken as the result of heat and constant stirring. While the filling simmers, prepare the biscuit topping.
6. Once the broth has completely thickened, add the heavy cream and peas into the mix. Bring the mixture to a simmer and then turn the heat down to low. Allow to simmer until the broth has the consistency of gravy. Season with salt and pepper if necessary.

For the topping:

1. In a medium-sized mixing bowl, whisk together the almond flour, xanthan gum, baking powder, flaxseed, and salt.
2. Add the butter in with the ingredients.
3. In a small bowl, add in the sour cream and egg white. Whisk the contents of the bowl

thoroughly and then pour into the bowl of dry ingredients.

4. Gather the mixture into the form of a ball and place it on a piece of parchment paper.

5. Using a rolling pin dusted with flour, roll the dough into a circle that is roughly 8 inches in diameter.

6. Pour the chicken filling into the prepared baking dish.

7. Gently place the dough over the chicken filling.

8. Bake in the oven for around 10 to 12 minutes or until the topping has browned.

Enjoy!

Brussel Sprouts and Bacon: Veggies with a Side of Bacon Goodness

As a child, you were probably encouraged by your elders to eat your vegetables. You likely have been told that eating lots of greens is going to help make you stronger and healthier. However, you also knew that eating junk food was much more delicious. You always found yourself gravitating towards the cookie jar as opposed to the plate of roasted brussel sprouts. However, now that you're older, you probably do realize the importance of eating healthier. But that still doesn't take away from the fact that cookies taste better than brussel sprouts. There's just no way for the converse to ever be true.

Or maybe you just aren't cooking brussel sprouts right. Again, the best way to enjoy the food that you eat is to be creative with it. With this recipe, brussel sprouts are going to take center stage. And it's guaranteed that you won't have to force yourself to eat your veggies this time around. It will actually be a genuine pleasure for you to do so. The bacon is only there as a form of added incentive for you to eat your veggies. The best part of this recipe is that it's incredibly simple and that it's keto-friendly.

Number of Servings: 4 servings

Preparation Time: 5 minutes

Cooking Time: 20 minutes

Macros per Serving:

- Fat: 19 g
- Protein: 6 g
- Carbohydrates: 11 g

Total Calories per Serving: 240 kcal

Ingredients:

- 4 slices thick-cut bacon
- 1 lb. brussel sprouts, sliced into halves
- 3 tbsp. virgin olive oil
- ¾ tsp salt
- ¼ tsp black pepper
- 2 tbsp. balsamic vinegar

Directions:

1. Prepare a large sauté pan and place it over a stove on medium heat. Allow the pan to heat up and add the bacon. Fry the slices of bacon on both sides until they're firm and crisp.
2. Remove the bacon and situate them on top of paper towels to remove any excess oil. However, do not remove the grease that is left in the pan.
3. Add olive oil to the pan, swirl it around, and let it mix with the bacon grease. Add the brussel sprouts into the pan and cook for a while. Season with salt and black pepper according to taste.
4. Bring the heat of the stove to medium-high. Arrange all of the sprouts in a single layer. Allow the brussel sprouts to sear for around 4 minutes or until it is browned on the bottom side. Flip the sprouts and allow to sear until the other side is browned as well.

5. While waiting for the sprouts to brown, chop the bacon slices.
6. Add balsamic vinegar and olive oil into the pan with the brussel sprouts. Cook for another 2 minutes.
7. Add the chopped bacon to the pan and toss everything together.

Enjoy!

Sesame Chicken: Asian Powerhouse the Keto Way

Chinese cuisine is amazing. There's a reason why Chinese cuisine continues to be one of the most celebrated cuisines in the world. Regardless of if it's high-end Chinese food reserved for the rich and affluent or if it's down-to-earth dumplings that you can find in the middle of Chinatown. There is a specific offering for everyone. Chinese cuisine is rich and vast in its history. It's not that hard to see why so many people love it. It's also the reason why Chinese restaurants seem to be popping up everywhere, constantly. Any modernized city in all parts of the world is bound to have a Chinese restaurant every few blocks or so.

However, Chinese food has had some kind of a bad reputation in the health and wellness industry. For one, most Chinese dishes contain MSG, which is incredibly high in sodium. Also, a lot of Chinese dishes are just loaded with sugar and soy. Part of what makes Chinese food so delicious is that there is an abundance of flavors that comes from so many different ingredients. However, it can be so easy to overindulge on Chinese food. That's why it's important to make sure that consumption of Chinese cuisine is kept to a minimum.

But when you've got a craving, then you've got a craving. Fortunately, there are recipes like this one that exist which are designed to satisfy those cravings without having to violate the principles of your diet. This recipe in particular is going to focus on a classic Chinese dish: sesame chicken. A great addition to any dinner table, this tangy and savory dish is going to be a big hit.

Number of Servings: 2 servings

Preparation Time: 15 minutes

Cooking Time: 15 minutes

Macros per Serving:

- Fat: 36 g
- Protein:45 g
- Carbohydrates: 4 g

Total Calories per Serving: 520 kcal

Ingredients:

For the chicken:

- 1 egg
- 1 tbsp. arrowroot powder (or cornstarch)
- 1 lb. chicken thigh meat
- 1 tbsp. toasted sesame oil
- Salt and pepper to taste

For the sesame sauce:

- 2 tbsp. soy sauce
- 1 tbsp. toasted sesame oil
- 1 tbsp. vinegar
- 2 tbsp. Sukrin Gold sweetener (or substitute)
- 1 cm cube of ginger
- 1 clove garlic
- 2 tbsp. sesame seeds
- ¼ tsp xanthan gum

Directions:

1. For the batter, prepare a large bowl and mix a large egg with a tablespoon of arrowroot powder.
2. Whisk the mixture thoroughly and add bite-sized pieces of chicken thigh meat. Make sure that all the pieces of chicken are thoroughly coated.
3. In a large pan, heat up a tablespoon of sesame seed oil. Slowly add the chicken thighs to the pan while making sure that there is space between every piece. If necessary, cook them in separate batches.
4. Be gentle as you flip the chicken meat to make sure that the breading doesn't separate from the chicken.
5. While the chicken meat is cooking, prepare the sesame sauce.
6. Combine all of the sauce ingredients into one bowl and mix well.
7. Once your chicken has finished cooking (approx. 10 minutes), add the sesame sauce into the pan and cook for another 5 minutes.
8. When the chicken is cooked, serve on a bed of steamed broccoli. Garnish with sesame seeds and green onion.

Enjoy!

Tofu Curry Scramble: A Hearty Breakfast Dish with a Kick!

This is a great breakfast that you can just whip up in a span of 30 minutes. For people who are looking to start their day with a healthy dose of protein, then this is definitely the recipe for you. You know that you aren't going to be short-changed when it comes to flavor on this dish. The different flavors that you get from the mushrooms, peppers, and onions are definitely going to make this dish a go-to for your morning meal.

It's such a refreshing feeling to be able to break your fast in the morning with a dish that is packed with protein, while being low in carbohydrates. Oh, and this dish happens to be gluten-free and vegan-friendly as well. That's why it's great for keto/vegan hybrid dieters who miss having scrambled eggs in the morning. This is just as good and it is just as healthy too.

Tofu can be really tricky to deal with sometimes. That's why you have to remind yourself of a few things before you try your hand at this dish. You have to press the tofu beforehand. It's important that the tofu is drained of water so that you won't end up with a soggy and squishy scramble. Also, when seasoning, try adding the spices directly onto the tofu. Tofu is a great receptor and absorber of spices. To maximize flavor, try to get the most out of the spices that you have on there.

Number of Servings: 4 servings

Preparation Time: 10 minutes

Cooking Time: 20 minutes

Macros per Serving:

- Fat: 5 g
- Protein: 11 g
- Carbohydrates: 9 g

Total Calories per Serving: 119 kcal

Ingredients:

For the tofu scramble:

- 1 block firm organic tofu, pressed and drained
- ½ medium-sized onion, diced
- 1 large red pepper, diced
- 6 oz. sliced mushrooms

- 3 tbsp. low-sodium vegetable broth
- 3 cups chopped greens (kale, spinach, arugula, etc.)

For the curry seasoning:

- ½ tsp of curry powder
- ½ tsp garlic powder
- ½ tsp cumin
- ¼ tsp paprika
- ¼ tsp coriander
- ¼ tsp turmeric
- ¼ tsp garam masala
- ¼ tsp salt
- 1 tbsp. water

Enjoy!

Low-Carb Salmon Wasabi Burgers: A Protein Feast with a Hint of Spice

If you are a lover of spicy food and fish, then you're going to adore this take on the salmon wasabi burger. You are definitely going to enjoy the strong aroma of wasabi and ginger meshing together and overloading your senses. Of course, the star of the meal is the protein: salmon. However, you can substitute the salmon with beef or chicken if that's more your thing. The wasabi is really just a kicker that's going to make you want to take bite after bite.

It should also be mentioned that these burgers don't need buns for you to enjoy them. That's why they're safe for a keto diet. However, you can also search for keto recipes that can teach you to make keto-friendly buns if you are one of those people who think that eating burgers without buns is sacrilege. If you're not one of those people, feel free to enjoy these burger patties with a side of vegetables or cauliflower rice.

Typically, you may also have a habit of dousing your burgers with all sorts of condiments like ketchup, mayonnaise, or mustard. You are free to do so on this burger patty. However, you don't really need to. The patties in themselves already pack a lot of flavor and it would be a shame to drown all of that flavor out with ketchup. If you're having some friends over for dinner, this would serve as a great treat for them as it's unlikely to be anything they've ever had before.

Number of Servings: 4 servings

Preparation Time: 5 minutes

Cooking Time: 10 minutes

Macros per Serving:

- Fat: 12 g
- Protein: 29 g
- Carbohydrates: 4 g

Total Calories per Serving: 320 kcal

Ingredients:

- 1 lb. skinless salmon fillet
- 1 tbsp. water
- 1 tbsp. freshly peeled and minced ginger
- ¼ cup minced cilantro
- ¼ cup chopped scallions

- 2 large eggs
- 1 tbsp. lime juice
- ½ cup blanched almond flour
- 1 tsp sea salt
- ¼ cup wasabi powder
- Coconut oil for frying

Directions:

1. Rinse the salmon and pat dry with a paper towel.
2. Slice the salmon into quarter-inch cubes.
3. In a large bowl, place the salmon, eggs, cilantro, lime juice, scallions, almond flour, and sea salt.
4. In a small bowl, combine wasabi powder and water to form wasabi paste.
5. Mix the wasabi paste together with the salmon mixture.
6. Form the batter into 2-inch patties.
7. Place a medium-sized skillet over medium-high heat and heat the oil.
8. Sauté the patties until the surface appears golden brown. This should take around 6 to 8 minutes per side.
9. Serve with salad greens or vegetables.

Enjoy!

Cauliflower Mac and Cheese: Keto's Take on a Cheesy and Indulgent Comfort Food

Who doesn't love mac and cheese? It's probably one of the most beloved foods in the world, to be honest. Even if you're just getting overly processed mac and cheese that comes from a box, it still manages to hit the spot. But of course, we're not going to be having anything like that for this particular recipe. First of all, mac and cheese that come from boxes are packed with lots of unwanted preservatives and sodium. Also, regular mac and cheese just has way too many carbohydrates. These carbs would definitely be enough to keep you from entering a state of ketosis for a whole day.

In this recipe, macaroni is going to be replaced by cauliflower, the keto wonder food. If you have read the entirety of this cookbook thus far, then you would know that cauliflower is a great substitute for rice. But now, you're about to learn that it can be a great substitute for macaroni as well. This keto mac and cheese recipe is going to taste so good that you won't even be able to tell the difference between this recipe and traditional mac and cheese. Also, as always, there are minimal carbs in this recipe and so you won't have to worry about your diet being wrecked by your cravings. Enjoy a piping hot serving of cheesy goodness with this mac and cheese recipe.

Number of Servings: 4 servings

Preparation Time: 5 minutes

Cooking Time: 20 minutes

Macros per Serving:

- Fat: 23 g
- Protein: 11 g
- Carbohydrates: 12 g

Total Calories per Serving: 294 kcal

Ingredients:

- 1 full head of cauliflower, sliced into smaller florets
- 3 tbsp. butter
- ¼ cup full cream
- 1 cup shredded cream cheese
- ¼ cup unsweetened almond milk
- Salt and pepper to taste

Directions:

1. Preheat oven to 450 degrees F or 230 degrees C and prepare a baking sheet lined with parchment paper.
2. Melt 2 tbsp. of butter on top of the stove. Transfer the melted butter into a bowl.

3. Take cauliflower florets and add them into a bowl with melted butter, salt, and pepper.
4. Place the cauliflower on top of the baking sheet and roast for approximately 15 minutes or until it begins to crisp.
5. Add shredded cheese, milk, and cream into a broiler and heat on top of the stove on medium-high heat. If you wish, you may also make use of a microwave for this step.
6. Heat the mixture until it achieves a smooth and bubbly consistency. Be very careful to not overcook the cheese to the point that it burns and starts to brown.
7. Toss cauliflower together with the cheese mixture and serve hot.

Enjoy!

Baked Garlic Butter Salmon: Garlic Buttery Goodness in Less Than 30 Minutes

Fish is always going to be one of the best sources of protein that you can have. It is incredibly high in protein so it can help to build and repair muscles. At the same time, it is very low in calories and unwanted fats. This means that you won't have to worry too much about eating too much of it. Also, fish has a lot of omega-3 fatty acids that can help the immune system and strengthen muscles and joints.

When it comes to fish, there are few things better than a nicely baked salmon drenched in garlic butter sauce. This dish is packed with a lot of flavor, and it's fairly simple to make. You get all of the nutritional benefits of eating fish while also enjoying the flavorful experience that comes with consuming a delicious piece of salmon. This recipe is designed to have you eating this dish in less than 30 minutes. So, whenever you're pressed for time and you're really hungry, then this recipe would be perfect for you.

You can also try making this dish in big batches, so it would just be a matter of reheating the salmon any time you feel hungry. Since salmon is such a healthy source of protein, it's always going to be a guilt-free dining experience for you. You don't need carbs for you to feel fulfilled and happy with what you're eating. This salmon recipe is proof of that.

Number of Servings: 4 servings

Preparation Time: 5 minutes

Cooking Time: 22 minutes

Macros per Serving:

- Fat: 24 g
- Protein: 37 g
- Carbohydrates: 6 g

Total Calories per Serving: 450 kcal

Ingredients:

- 1 ½ lbs. salmon fillet, sliced in 4 equal parts
- ¼ cup butter
- 3 cloves minced garlic
- 2 tbsp chopped parsley
- 1 tsp lemon zest
- 1 lb. cauliflower florets
- Lemon wedges
- Salt and pepper to taste

Directions:

1. Preheat the oven to 400 degrees F or 205 degrees C.
2. Prepare a baking sheet and place 2 tbsp of butter on it. Place the baking sheet in the oven as it preheats.
3. Take the remaining butter and allow to melt by microwaving it, or place it on the stove for a few seconds. Make sure to not burn the butter.

4. In a small bowl, whisk together the melted butter, parsley, garlic, and lemon zest.
5. Remove the baking sheet from the oven and add cauliflower on top of it. Season with salt and pepper to taste. Bake for 10 minutes.
6. Remove the baking sheet from the oven once more and maneuver the florets around to make space for the salmon fillets. Season the fillets with garlic butter, salt, and pepper to taste.
7. Bake the fish for another 10 to 12 minutes or until the meat becomes slightly opaque. The length of baking depends on the thickness of the fillet.
8. Serve the salmon hot with lemon wedges for additional flavor.

Enjoy!

Bacon and Shrimp Chowder: Creamy Bowl of Warmth and Happiness

If you want to talk about comfort food, then you have to include a good bowl of soup in the discussion. Naturally, there is a reason why we always serve soup to our loved ones who are feeling sick and under the weather. It's easy. It's convenient. It's satisfying. It is really hard to go wrong with a nice bowl of soup, especially when you're not up for eating anything too heavy or complicated. That's why this recipe really hits the spot.

As simple as it might be to make, there are a lot of flavors and textures involved that will make the dish interesting to eat. With shrimp and bacon serving as its base, this recipe is packed with protein. The added Cajun seasoning is also going to give a little extra kick to the dish. However, be careful to add Cajun seasoning that doesn't have salt in it. Otherwise, you might be better off not adding any extra salt to your recipe after. Be prepared for the soup to dance on your taste buds a little bit before you take your next bite.

Chowder is often served in huge bread bowls. However, we need to ensure this chowder stays keto-friendly, so you're just going to have to make do with regular bowls. Also, all of the ingredients in this recipe are keto-friendly, so you won't have to beat yourself up for eating it. Also, if you make this in big batches, you can always refrigerate the leftovers and reheat for whenever you're looking for a quick snack.

Number of Servings: 6 servings

Preparation Time: 5 minutes

Cooking Time: 25 minutes

Macros per Serving:

- Fat: 32 g
- Protein: 16.5 g
- Carbohydrates: 5.5 g

Total Calories per Serving: 390 kcal

Ingredients:

- 6 slices chopped thick-cut bacon
- 1 lb. peeled and deveined shrimp
- 2 cups chicken broth

- 1 medium-sized turnip, chopped into ½ inch cubes
- ½ cup chopped onion
- 1 cup heavy cream
- ½ tsp Cajun seasoning
- Salt and pepper to taste
- Chopped parsley (for garnish)

Directions:

1. Prepare a large pan and place it over medium heat. Place the chopped bacon on the pan and cook until crisp. Once the bacon has finished cooking, remove the meat from the pan and place on a plate lined with a paper towel. Don't remove the leftover bacon grease from the pan.

2. With the bacon grease still hot, add the chopped turnip and onion to the pan. Sauté until the onions become tender. This should take around 5 minutes or so. Add the garlic to the pan and cook for another minute or until it becomes fragrant. Pour the chicken broth into the pan and allow to simmer for 10 minutes. The simmering process should tenderize the turnip.

3. Once the turnip is soft, add the cream into the pan along with the shrimps. Simmer until the shrimp becomes a pink or orange color. This should take around 3 minutes or

so. Season with Cajun seasoning, salt, and pepper.

4. Garnish the shrimp with the chopped bacon and parsley upon serving.

Enjoy!

Salad in a Jar: A Healthy and Filling Lunch for the Person on The Go

Sometimes, you just don't want to have to think about what to eat when you're hungry. Imagine waking up late to work in the morning. You know that you have limited time to prepare yourself for the long day ahead. However, you also know that you need to have your fill at midday to avoid overeating throughout the latter portion of the day. With this, you end up looking for something that is quick and easy to make. Also, it would be really helpful if this were a dish that you could take with you; a kind of meal that you could still eat while you're on the move. This is where this recipe comes in. The salad jar is perfect for the healthy eater who just wants a quick, easy, and convenient way to eat food while staying mobile, active, and on schedule

Another great thing about this recipe is how flexible it is. For this recipe, in particular, you are going to use delicious rotisserie chicken as your protein. However, you can always substitute this with any protein source that you like. You can also make use of flaked tuna, smoked salmon, grilled shrimp, shredded pork, or whatever else you may think of. The possibilities are endless. Diversity and variation are important aspects of a dish like this so that you don't end up getting bored with your diet. Mix things up every so often so that things don't stay repetitive and predictable with what you eat. Aside from diversifying your use of major proteins, you can also incorporate nuts, cheese cubes, and seeds into the dish for another layer of complexity.

Number of Servings: 1 serving or 1 jar

Preparation Time: 5 minutes

Cooking Time: 0 minutes

Macros per Serving:

- Fat: 84 g
- Protein: 75 g
- Carbohydrates: 11 g

Total Calories per Serving: 1133 kcal

Ingredients:

- 4 oz. rotisserie chicken, shredded

- 1 oz. green leafy vegetables (spinach, lettuce, cabbage, kale)
- ½ scallion, sliced
- 1 medium-sized avocado
- 1 oz. red bell peppers
- 1 oz. cherry tomatoes
- ¼ cup mayonnaise or extra virgin olive oil
- 1 carrot

Directions:

1. Shred or chop all of the vegetables by hand or with a machine.
2. Layer the jar by laying down a base of green leafy vegetables at the bottom.
3. For subsequent layers, it's up to you. However, the suggested order is as follows: scallions, carrots, avocados, bell peppers, and tomatoes.
4. Add the protein on top of all of the layers of vegetables.
5. Top the jar with mayonnaise or olive oil according to your preference.

Enjoy!

Keto-Friendly Chicken Quesadillas: Get Lit Up by These Chicken Quesadi-YAAAS!

As has already been established in our recipe for keto beef tacos, it can be really hard to resist a delicious Mexican dish. Somehow, even when you eat a taco or a burrito from a random hole in the wall, it's still pretty good. That's because it can be really hard to go wrong with meat and cheese. For the most part, this is a combo that always works regardless of whatever you choose to do with it. That's why it's going to be really easy for you to make this recipe, as well. We're going back with the tried and tested combo of meat and cheese to offer you a gastronomic experience that is both heartwarming and comforting.

Traditionally, quesadillas are loaded with carbs because of the tortillas that are used to make them. These tortillas usually sandwich some mixture of cheese and some kind of protein like beef, chicken, or pork. These quesadillas are usually enjoyed with cheese along with a side of tomato salsa for some added flavor. However, we aren't going to be making use of typical tortillas for this recipe. In lieu of flour tortillas, you can make use of keto-friendly crust alternatives such as almond, zucchini, or cauliflower-based crusts. It's important that you are still able to stay in ketosis even if you indulge in your favorite Mexican treats. Here is a quick and easy Mexican chicken quesadilla that you can make in your sleep. It's perfect for when you have a craving that just won't go away even when you're trying to stick to a strict keto diet.

Number of Servings: 4 servings

Preparation Time: 15 minutes

Cooking Time: 20 minutes

Macros per Serving:

- Fat: 26 g
- Protein: 29 g
- Carbohydrates: 5 g

Total Calories per Serving: 410 kcal

Ingredients:

- 2 chicken thigh fillets, chopped into ½ inch pieces
- 2 keto-friendly crusts
- 1 tbsp taco seasoning
- 2 medium-sized green onions, thinly sliced
- ½ medium-sized green bell pepper, sliced into ½ inch pieces
- 1 ½ cups shredded cheddar cheese
- 2 tbsp avocado oil
- Salt and pepper to taste

Directions:

1. Prepare a large skillet and place it over medium heat. Add one tablespoon of avocado oil to the pan and heat until it begins to simmer. However, don't let it get too hot to the point where it starts to smoke.

2. Add chicken to the pan and allow to heat up until it cooks all the way through. This should take around 5 minutes or so. Sprinkle taco seasoning on the chicken and toss.

3. Add the pepper and onions to the pot and stir thoroughly. Cook for around 3 to 5 minutes or until the vegetables are tender.

4. Transfer the chicken and vegetables to a large bowl and set aside. Wipe the pan clean with a paper towel. Add another half

tablespoon of olive oil and then reduce the heat to a medium low.

5. Add one pizza crust to the pan and shower it with ½ cup of cheese. Take around half of the chicken filling and spread it around the crust over the cheese. Shower another ¼ cup of cheese on top of the chicken and then top it with the second layer of pizza crust.

6. Cover the pan and then cook until the cheese has completely melted and the bottom of the crust has browned. This should only take around 2 to 4 minutes. Carefully flip the crust over and cook the other side for another 2 minutes. Remove the crust from the pan and allow to cool slightly before slicing.

7. Repeat the same process with the remainder of crusts and filling.

Enjoy!

Cheesy Breakfast Omelet: A Cheesy Start to the Day

They say that breakfast is the most important meal of the day. And it's really not all that hard to figure out why. You want to be able to start your day feeling refreshed and energized. That's why it's essential that you are able to get all the nutrients required into your system to help fuel you to dominate the rest of the day. When you don't start off the day feeling good, it can really set the tone for what the rest of your day is going to be like. Never underestimate the power of breakfast! However, a lot of people who are on boring and bland diets will settle for plain boiled eggs and a piece of toast for breakfast. Not that there's anything wrong with that if you find that meal enjoyable, but there's always going to be a lot of room for more options.

This playful and delightful recipe for a cheesy breakfast omelet is perfect for keto practitioners because it doesn't violate ketosis, and it carries a lot of healthy fats and proteins to help keep you full and energized. Also, it's fairly easy to make. So, whenever you wake up in the morning and aren't really in the mood to make anything too complicated, then this should be a go-to recipe for you. Eggs carry a lot of antioxidants, healthy fats, and protein to keep you feeling strong, and cheese is going to be a great source of comfort for anyone.

Number of Servings: 2 servings

Preparation Time: 2 minutes

Cooking Time: 4 to 6 minutes

Macros per Serving:

- Fat: 80 g
- Protein: 40 g
- Carbohydrates: 4 g

Total Calories per Serving: 900 kcal

Ingredients:

- 6 medium-sized eggs
- 7 oz. shredded cheddar cheese
- 3 oz. butter at room temperature
- Salt and pepper to taste

Directions:

1. Crack the eggs into a large bowl and whisk together until it becomes smooth and frothy. Add half of the prepared cheddar cheese to the bowl and mix with the egg until it is spread out evenly.
2. Place a pan over medium-low heat and melt the butter into the pan. Spread the butter evenly so that it covers the entire surface. Slowly add the eggs into the pan and continuously stir while cooking. Once the bottom of the eggs have browned and hardened, add the remaining cheese on top.
3. Fold the egg once to sandwich the cheese. Cook for another few seconds to allow the cheese to melt.
4. Season with salt and pepper.

Enjoy!

Keto Tuna Patties: A Tuna-rrific Patty!

When it comes to healthy food, a nice serving of canned tuna is great for people who just want an accessible and convenient source of protein. However, let's face the truth, tuna can be bland if you don't cook it right. A lot of people are quick to just toss the tuna into a pan, add a few spices, and then eat it. While that's okay, it can also get boring. Pretty soon, you're going to end up getting sick of tuna and you will want to revert to other sources of protein. Fortunately, this recipe is looking to shake things up a little. You will discover that canned tuna doesn't always have to be such a boring food item by the time you finish trying this amazing take on tuna patties.

They're so delicious that you won't have any troubles getting your kids to eat more fish. Tuna is a great source of lean protein and omega-3 fatty acids. That means that this is a recipe that's great for family dinners and get-togethers. Also, it's perfect for keto practitioners because the patties only have 2 grams of carbs per serving. Add the extra kick of flavor from lemon and dill to make this dish a new favorite for everyone in the household. Even if you're not the biggest fan of tuna as a protein, you can always take this recipe and substitute the tuna with cooked shredded chicken. It all works the same.

Number of Servings: 8 patties

Preparation Time: 10 minutes

Cooking Time: 10 minutes

Macros per Serving:

- Fat: 14 g
- Protein: 22 g
- Carbohydrates: 2 g

Total Calories per Serving: 215 kcal

Ingredients:

- 20 oz. canned tuna, drained
- ⅓ cup almond flour
- 2 tbsp chopped fresh dill
- 2 medium-sized green onions, chopped
- 1 tbsp lemon zest
- ¼ cup mayonnaise
- 1 large egg
- 2 tbsp avocado oil
- 1 tbsp lemon juice
- Salt and pepper to taste

Directions:

1. In a large bowl, combine all of the ingredients except for the avocado oil. Stir the entire mixture thoroughly until everything is well-combined. Then, divide the mixture into 8 equal parts and form patties about ¾ inch thick.

2. Prepare a large skillet and place it over medium heat. Add the avocado oil and allow to heat until it starts simmering. Add around half of the tuna patties and cook until golden brown. Make sure that the patties don't come into contact with one another. Once the bottom of the patties are browned, flip, and repeat the process on the other side. This should take around 3 to 4 minutes on each side.

3. Remove the patties and place it on top of a plate lined with a paper towel to absorb the excess oil. Repeat the same process with the remaining patties.

4. Top the patties with lemon and mayo as garnish.

Enjoy!

Deviled Eggs: A Fiery Treat for the Keto Dieter

Whether you just want to have a delicious snack ready at home for whenever you're hungry or if you're looking to host a party for friends at your place, this recipe is going to come in handy for you. Deviled eggs are always going to be a prominent feature at any potluck or party. They're interesting to look at, and they're pretty tasty too. Of course, this keto variation is going to offer all of that great flavor without any of the unwanted carbs that can take you out of your state of ketosis. Sometimes, you just want to be able to go to your fridge and grab a quick bite to eat without having to prepare anything. These deviled eggs are great for that purpose. After preparing them, you can just leave them in your fridge for whenever you get hungry in the future. They also make for great appetizers at dinners and social gatherings.

Of course, the base of the recipe will be the eggs. But eggs on their own can get really bland and boring. That's why a protein like peeled shrimp or smoked salmon can also be incorporated into the mix. For this recipe in particular, we will be making use of peeled shrimp. Add just a hint of tabasco to each deviled egg for some added spice and complexity to the flavor of the dish. Oh, and the best part? There is less than 1 gram of carbs per serving.

Number of Servings: 4 servings

Preparation Time: 5 minutes

Cooking Time: 10 minutes

Macros per Serving:

- Fat: 15 g
- Protein: 7 g
- Carbohydrates: 0.5 g

Total Calories per Serving: 163 kcal

Ingredients:

- 4 medium eggs
- 1 tsp tabasco hot sauce
- ¼ cup mayonnaise
- 8 pieces cooked and peeled shrimp
- Fresh dill
- Salt and pepper to taste

Directions:

1. Begin by placing all of the eggs into a large pot. Add enough water until all of the eggs are submerged and cover the pot. Place the pot over medium heat and bring the water to a boil.
2. Boil the eggs for around 8 to 10 minutes to make sure that they are hard boiled.
3. After the eggs have fully hardened, remove the eggs from the pot and place in an ice bath for a few minutes. Allow the eggs to cool for a little bit before peeling.
4. Split the eggs in half crosswise and remove the yolks. Place the yolks in a medium-sized bowl.

5. Set the egg whites aside on a separate plate.
6. Mash the yolks in the bowl and add the salt, Tabasco, and mayonnaise.
7. Using a spoon, add small scoops of the yolk mixtures into the hollowed egg whites. Top the yolk with shrimp.
8. Add fresh dill to garnish.

Enjoy!

Bacon-Wrapped Cheese Sticks: Loaded Sticky Bombs

If you've been on the keto diet for a while, then you're probably seeing a theme here. Cheese tends to be a staple ingredient in the diet plans of a lot of keto practitioners. It's just really delicious, isn't it? Except for people who are lactose-intolerant, cheese is a really good source of comfort and satisfaction for a lot of people who are looking for a good bite to eat. In fact, even people who are lactose-intolerant would be willing to risk a night of being sick just to get a taste of some amazing cheesy foods. And it's likely that this cheese stick recipe is really going to test the discipline of these lactose-intolerant individuals. Fortunately, for lactose-tolerant keto practitioners, it's a delicious indulgence that you don't have to fear or be guilty about.

Oh, and did we forget to mention that bacon is also involved? Usually, when you make cheese sticks in a traditional sense, you add breadcrumbs to the skin to preserve the integrity of the cheese stick. However, breadcrumbs are a big no-no for keto dieters. Fortunately, this recipe definitely does away with the breadcrumbs, and instead, uses a great alternative – bacon. Bacon is another one of those foods that just bring a lot of comfort and joy to a lot of people.

For this recipe, in particular, you're going to be making use of the oven to bake the cheese sticks. However, you should know that you can also make use of a frying pan if you don't have access to an oven or if you just don't want to use one.

You're probably salivating by now, so let's get right to the recipe.

Number of Servings: 2 servings

Preparation Time: 5 minutes

Cooking Time: 10 minutes

Macros per Serving:

- Fat: 61 g
- Protein: 34 g
- Carbohydrates: 4 g

Total Calories per Serving: 705 kcal

Ingredients:

- 8 oz. halloumi cheese
- 6 oz. thin-cut bacon slices

Directions:

1. Preheat the oven to 450 degrees F or 225 degrees C.
2. Cut the cheese into 8 to 10 evenly segmented pieces.
3. Wrap a slice of bacon around each piece of cheese. Try to cover as much cheese as possible to prevent it from melting over.
4. Prepare a baking sheet lined with parchment paper. Place the cheese sticks onto the baking sheet.
5. Place the baking sheet into the oven and bake for around 10 to 15 minutes or until they become golden brown. Flip the sticks halfway through baking.

Enjoy!

Keto Chicken Caprese: A Filling and Fanciful Keto Treat

This might be a loaded thing to say, but this quick and easy recipe for keto chicken caprese is probably going to end up being one of your most favorite meals to make. For one, it's really simple to execute. You won't have to stress yourself trying to get things just right to get this dish to taste good. And going off of that, the dish is just absolutely delicious. You start out with five very simple ingredients. and you're able to make something that tastes fanciful and luxurious. In fact, you might end up feeling like you're eating at a fancy restaurant. Also, one of the best parts of this recipe is just how unpretentious it is. It's likely that every member of your family is going to love having this, should you ever choose to prepare it as the main course for a family dinner.

The chicken is going to serve as the base for this dish. And as you may already know, chicken is a great source of protein. This means that this would make a great dish for athletes who are looking for a high protein meal to help build muscle. But this would also be a great dish for kids who need protein to get bigger and stronger. At the end of the day, you can never go wrong with chicken. Of course, the protein is only going to be accentuated by the deliciousness of the cheese and the freshness of the tomatoes and basil. Lastly, the best part of this dish is that it barely has 1 gram of carbs per serving. To really get this dish to taste great, try to ensure that your ingredients are as fresh as possible.

Number of Servings: 4 servings

Preparation Time: 5 minutes

Cooking Time: 35 minutes

Macros per Serving:

- Fat: 19 g
- Protein: 36 g
- Carbohydrates: 1 g

Total Calories per Serving: 315 kcal

Ingredients:

- 5 chicken thigh fillets
- 6 oz. sliced mozzarella cheese
- 1 medium-sized tomatoes, sliced

- 2 tbsp avocado oil
- ¼ cup chopped basil
- Salt and pepper to taste

Directions:

1. Preheat the oven to 375 degrees F or 190 degrees C.
2. Prepare a large skillet and place it over medium heat. Add the avocado oil to the skillet and allow to heat until it begins to simmer. Season the chicken thighs with salt and pepper and add it into the skillet. Sear the fillets on one side until it browns. Then, flip it and sear the other side until it reaches the same kind of brownness. This should take around 2 to 3 minutes per side.
3. Arrange the chicken thigh fillets in a single layer in a glass baking dish. Top each fillet with a single slice of mozzarella and a single slice of tomato on top of the cheese.
4. Place the baking pan into the oven and bake for around 25 to 28 minutes. Toward the end, the cheese should start to melt and bubble. At that point, turn the broiler on for 2 to 3 minutes to slightly brown the cheese. Make sure to not overcook the cheese to the point where it burns.
5. Remove the chicken from the oven and garnish with fresh basil.

Enjoy!

Stuffed Mushroom Snackers: A Healthy Treat for the Constant Snacker

Let's face it. There are a lot of us who just love to snack. A lot of the time, people gain weight when they don't control the number of calories that they consume on a daily basis. This can be easily dealt with by merely adjusting portion size during the main meals of the day. However, for most people, the calories come throughout the course of the day in the form of snacks. Sure, you might have fruit for breakfast, but then you reach right for that bag of Cheetos midway through the afternoon. Obviously, snacking can be a very dangerous habit. But the biggest problem with snacking is that it's not easy to stop. In fact, a lot of people can just mindlessly snack on random food without even giving it a second thought. This is when all of those calories add up and can lead to weight gain.

That's why when you're on a diet, you have to make sure that you are staying mindful of your snacking habits. You will want to limit snacking as much as possible to avoid taking in bad calories.

However, if you can't kick the habit, you can resort to healthier options for your snacks. That is precisely where this recipe comes in. Whether you're practicing keto or not, this recipe is going to be great for you. You can prepare a huge bunch of mushroom snackers and store them in the fridge for whenever you're hungry. They make for great appetizers when you're entertaining a large group of people at your home as well. There are essentially three main ingredients here: bacon, mushrooms, and cheese. The rest of the ingredients are just designed to further highlight the richness of the cheese, the saltiness of the bacon, and the texture of the mushroom.

Number of Servings: 4 servings

Preparation Time: 5 minutes

Cooking Time: 20 minutes

Macros per Serving:

- Fat: 46 g
- Protein: 12 g
- Carbohydrates: 5 g

Total Calories per Serving:

Ingredients:

- 8 oz. chopped bacon

- 12 portobello mushrooms
- 7 oz. cream cheese
- 2 tbsp butter
- 3 tbsp chopped chives
- 1 tsp paprika powder
- Salt and pepper to taste

Directions:

1. Preheat the oven to 400 degrees F or 200 degrees C.
2. Prepare a frying pan and place it over medium-high heat. While waiting for the pan to get hot, chop the bacon up into small bits and pieces. Add the bacon to the pan and fry it until the bacon bits become very crispy.
3. Remove the bacon from the pan and add to another plate, but keep the bacon fat.
4. Prepare the mushrooms by removing the stems and chopping them finely. Sauté the mushroom stems in the bacon fat. Add butter if necessary.
5. While the mushroom stems are cooking, prepare a baking dish and grease it. Once the dish is fully greased, place the mushroom heads into the baking dish.
6. In a large bowl, mix the bacon bits and chopped mushroom stems along with the

other remaining ingredients. Scoop the fillings into each mushroom.

7. Bake for 20 minutes or until the mushrooms begin to brown.

Enjoy!

Keto Hot Chocolate: Keto Comfort in a Cup

For the final recipe on this list, let's mix things up a little bit. Instead of preparing a typical meal for the keto practitioner, we're going to do a little reimagining of a classic drink instead. Hot cocoa is something that many people tend to turn to whenever they're feeling a little chilly or under the weather. Of course, it's not all too hard to see why this would be one of those go-to comfort classics for people. It's essentially chocolate in hot liquid form. There's just something so comforting about a steamy chocolate flavored drink.

However, we all know that typical chocolate is laden with too much sugar and carbohydrates. This is why a lot of keto practitioners are nostalgic when they are on low-carb diets. They would end up missing the carb-filled comforts of hot chocolate, especially during the colder seasons. Well, with this recipe, you can turn your nostalgia into a reality. Enjoy a hot cup of cocoa and relax knowing that you aren't going to be compromising your ketogenic state. A single serving of this keto hot cocoa will have less than 200 calories!

Number of Servings: 4 servings

Preparation Time: 5 minutes

Cooking Time: 5 minutes

Macros per Serving:

- Fat: 18 g
- Protein: 2 g
- Carbohydrates: 4 g

Total Calories per Serving: 193 kcal

Ingredients:

- 6 oz. unsweetened, sugar-free dark chocolate
- ½ cup unsweetened almond milk
- ½ cup heavy cream
- ½ tsp vanilla extract
- 1 tbsp. Erythritol or any keto-friendly sweetener (optional)

Directions:

1. Prepare a saucepan and place it over medium heat.
2. Add the almond milk, cream, and sweetener of choice to the saucepan and heat until it simmers. Once it begins to simmer, remove the pan from the heat.

3. Stir in the vanilla extract and chocolate into the mixture and combine all ingredients thoroughly.
4. Pour the chocolate into espresso cups to serve.

Enjoy!

Conclusion

At the end of the day, the road to health and wellness is a long and winding one. You aren't necessarily going to have the easiest of times. No one is going to guarantee that you will find immediate success or if you're even going to find any success at all. However, as long as you do things right and if your heart is in the right place, you are definitely going to get a sense of fulfillment out of it. Not a lot of people realize that the most important investment that we can make is on our own personal health and wellness. Lots of people will say that dieting and eating healthy food is expensive. Well, that may very well be the case. However, the money that you spend on making healthy choices costs nothing if you compare it to the kind of money that you spend on medical bills if you get sick as a result of living unhealthily. Ultimately, being healthy is a state of mind. As cliché as it sounds, your health isn't determined by the grand decisions that you make. Your health and fitness are made up of the little choices that you make on a daily basis. Whether or not you get up early to run a 5k is your choice. Whether or not you forego that slice of chocolate cake for a cup of tea is your choice. It's little decisions like these that ultimately shape the state of your overall health and wellness.

Make no doubt about it. Getting fit and healthy is as complicated as things can possibly get. There are so many variables that come into play and there are a lot of things that you need to stay mindful of. However, the one area where you can't allow yourself to screw up is with your nutrition. It's very important that you pay close attention to the food that you eat on a daily basis. Sure, this cookbook might be advocating for keto recipes. But at the end of the day, you need to find a diet that works best for you. And if it just so happens that you find the most enjoyment and success under the keto lifestyle, then hopefully this book will have helped you to a certain extent.

One of the biggest challenges that people face while dieting is actually cooking. The truth is, the best way for you to pay attention to the food that you're eating is to cook your food yourself. However, not all people are going to be gifted with world-class culinary skills. And not all people are going to have the practical resources to have their meals prepared for them by a dedicated chef. This is precisely why this cookbook (and many others like it) exists. It's dedicated to people who are looking to stay healthy without having to concern themselves with complicated culinary principles.

You don't have to have the fanciest kitchen equipment out there. The recipes highlighted in this book can be executed with average household equipment. You shouldn't have to resort to feel intimidated by complex recipes on your road to health and wellness. The food that you eat should be the least of your worries.

The very fact that you have picked up a book like this is a victory in itself. It shows that you have felt a general discontent with the state of your life and your nutrition. And it also shows that you have a willingness to try to improve your state of life. Given that, you have already made substantial progress. You have already taken a step forward toward becoming the person you want to be. Hopefully, you will have gathered substantial information from this book that could help you achieve your personal goals and dreams for yourself.

To the majority of us, food is perceived as a source of comfort. It's more than just something that we need to consume in order to survive. Food is an entity that is powerful enough to define cultures and bring people together. The relationship that people have with food is always going to be important. And in order for your diet to be sustainable, it's important that you actually enjoy the food that you eat and that you find fulfillment in it. Sure, you can probably stick it out for a few days if you're on a diet that you don't enjoy. However, when it comes to staying healthy for years to come, it's very important that your relationship with food is a healthy and sustainable one. So, even though you need to be paying close attention to what you're eating, you shouldn't be depriving yourself of the joy that food can bring either. That's why cookbooks like this can really help you when you're on a diet. Being on keto doesn't mean that you don't have the privilege of enjoying your meals anymore.

Again, the road to getting fit and healthy isn't an easy one. But hopefully, this cookbook will help make that process easier, more enjoyable, and a lot tastier.